CAPSULE STORIES

Masthead
Natasha Lioe, Founder and Publisher
Carolina VonKampen, Publisher and Editor in Chief
April Bayer, Reader
Stephanie Coley, Reader
Rhea Dhanbhoora, Reader
Hannah Fortna, Reader
Kendra Nuttall, Reader
Rachel Skelton, Reader
Deanne Sleet, Reader
Claire Taylor, Reader

Cover art by Darius Serebrova
Book design by Carolina VonKampen

Paperback ISBN: 978-1-953958-04-4
Ebook ISBN: 978-1-953958-05-1

CAPSULE STORIES

Summer 2021 Edition

Contents

Letter from the Editors

We begin *Capsule Stories Summer 2021 Edition* with these words from Isabella J Mansfield's poem "The Things We Know Are There Even When We Cannot See":

> *sometimes we don't say*
> *the words, because*
> *we already know them*

So much has been written about the night sky over the millennia. We wanted to capture that feeling of awe and wonder that comes from staring up at the stars and exploring your deepest thoughts, and the world beyond yourself. In this edition, you'll read about taking the long way home at night so you can gaze up at the night sky. Staring up at the stars and feeling a pang of longing in your chest for the person you love. Looking at the stars as a kid and thinking how big and exciting the universe was. Looking at the stars as a grownup and feeling small. The stories and poems in this edition give us the words for these feelings that we already know deeply but don't always know how to say.

Starry Nights

You are lying on the beach, squinting up at the night sky. Voices sound close but feel far away. There are things you cannot control: the orbit of your rock around the sun, how the clouds cast shadows in the sand, how the sky lights up when the planet's star disappears beyond the horizon. You think about yourself and how you are just a tiny organism who made a home on a floating rock in space. When you look across the water, you can see the stars shining back at you. You think about how weird it is that the stars have been there the whole day, invisible, hiding in plain sight. Sometimes, you imagine yourself in the middle of the ocean, lying on your back, staring up at the stars. You are alone, thinking of the people who have led you here, and your problems become insignificant. As the water wraps around you like a blanket, you realize you are not alone—the stars have been there all along.

The Things We Know Are There Even When We Cannot See

Isabella J Mansfield

---

light pollution blots out stars
whose names
I have never known

somewhere, thunderheads
are sweeping in against
a blue-black sky

we sit here with bare limbs
tangled, listening to rain
beat against glass and steel

sometimes we don't say
the words, because
we already know them

Night Dive

Emily L. Pate

Dark falls first
on the ocean, our dive boat
anchored in the last memory
of sun as we strap BCDs on,
take a quick breath of bottled air,
check gauges. Then the backward
water-bound leap, hand holding breath
to my face until all I taste is salt
and rubber and the surface becomes
another galaxy. I drift down into night
of a different breed, stars gone. Here is the infinity
of the planetarium, the endless other side
of a telescope. All I see of my father is his T-shirt,
the drifting white of his sleeves, until
we twist flashlights on. Life awakes
in a circle of fluorescence, an eye
sent out by battery. Fireworms cyclone in the glow.
Red-spindle legs catch a dart of scaled blue
and drag into shadow. An octopus shifts orange,
arms curled, eyes alien and unblinking. Time slips soft
into the dark as I breathe through my carried air,
until we circle back to boat's anchor
and kneel in thirty-foot down sand. We switch off
our flashlights and night drifts in.
My bare arm brushes my father's,
ghosts elbow to elbow, painted green.
Strings of aurora chase my hands,
weaving nebulas, the ocean bioluminescent
in movement's aftermath. Then the rise,
the wait as breath inside my lungs forgets

depth. Surface. A jellyfish nettles my leg,
a small, stinging pain, and the ocean lifts me,
here at the horizon where water and sky are the same
gentle creature, eternity brought to rest in my eye.
My father touches his hand to my elbow,
tilts back his head, and just says
stars.

time slips soft into the dark

Evening in the Shadow of Mount Diablo

Emily L. Pate

Day ends summer-slow, heat in full-tide ebb
across the hill. Evening softens her palms
to my shoulders and invites me to the backyard,
where the frogs start to call all at once from the creek,
a swelling thrum of hiccupped song. Wind trembles
the oak tree into full body sway, leaves catching
pale green and gold. Tree-shadows drift across the pool,
turning it to reflection. Tucked up against the gravel
that once held slide and swing and tugboat-shaped sandbox,
the lemon trees sag to ripeness. Softball-size citrus fall
to the lawn, ready victims to night-running rats
who gnaw yellow from the peels and leave lemons naked
against grass and early rot. Incoming night is all silhouette,
sun submerging and the sky so pale it looks a backdrop,
the oak cut out dark against it, inverted to Lichtenberg scar.
Bats wing from tree to tree, paper-delicate, small sails
unfolding and holding and folding into shadow. Wind catches
the oak tree again and life all at once takes hold of me
and stills something I didn't know was running.

i listen,
still, for the
sound of
the train in
the summer

Vic Nogay

---

under an august full moon, we looked like spirits in the night—
fuzzy, formless to any watching eyes. our bodies lingered after
themselves like smoke in the wind, a gossamer brushstroke.
constellations hooked their skeleton arms into the road-worn
hems of our once-white skirts, lacing us into the goldenrod
and aster, graying in the dark.

when we reached the train, we stood back from the tracks,
paused to watch metal in motion. the force of it repelled us
like anti-gravity—we fell into the weeds, tumbling with the
bugs. supine, holding hands, we listened to the reverb of the
train, of the song, of the summer, of the end.

and still we listened
for what's sacred in the dark
once all'd gone quiet

no point in keeping secrets

Vic Nogay

if i could rewrite that night i spent with you in the woods somewhere in the appalachian foothills in a summer so hot the earth wheezed when the sun went down and steam pooled above the blacktop making rivers of the air, i would give in to you running your cool fingers up and down my bare arms, give in to your mouth on my inner thigh, give in to us, just kids, trying, but that night i felt your restraint, too; i wish you would have given in first so i could have made you feel my body ringing beneath the surface of my skin, quaking the roots of the tree where we slept, shaking the buckeyes loose from above, ushering in low rumbles from a distant storm, my ears swelling and blistering while you sang into my open mouth, too hot to hear a thing.

.soft
.process

AJ Buckle

---

everything was bathed in
purple and sweat and hot

breath and all of it repeated in
miniature on the dip between

your clavicle and shoulder. the
shadows on the wall were perfect

like the teardrop shape of your
breast. you'd pulled the curtain

back just enough to see the stars
in the summer sky and i traced the

line of Cassiopeia on the small of
your back. your lips tasted like

red wine. in that moment all i wanted
to do was ask if we should have just

collided and burst into atomic dust.
but i didn't because i had no idea

what i'd have done if you said yes.
i don't want much, i just wanted to

become nebulae with you. in that
moment we could have been perfect

i watch it all from a distance now,
because i haunt myself. i can't help it.

Stranger Lights

Pamela Nocerino

A night rose
lit by a passing car
stirs an ache,
so the edges of me
lean in
and wait
to view again
the impermanent
secret glow
of blooming
in darkness

After Oysters and Jazz @ 2 a.m.

Pamela Nocerino

My forearm
rests in pretend casual
out the open driver's window
as I pull away,

and you touch it
in a desperate surprise,

igniting need
I never knew
and a symphony of longing
I've never answered.

First Date Sonata

Emily Polson

I. Introduction

I'll walk north on Prospect Park West, he messages.
   I'll walk south and meet you halfway.
   I'll be the guy with the cliché New Yorker *tote.*
   I smile. *We'll match.*

II. First Movement

I'll paint the scene a few minutes later: I stride forward on the double-laned sidewalk, a green wall of trees to my left, honking cars to my right, and straight ahead my date in a pastel pink button-down, the sleeves rolled up to his elbows. He smiles, waves, then makes a playful gesture to our bags. This might have been a meet-cute right out of an indie flick, if we hadn't met on an app. My life directed by Noah Baumbach.

"After you," he says. "This is your part of Brooklyn."

But this side of the park is unfamiliar to me. I suggested meeting at the northernmost tip of the diamond in front of its crowning jewel, the gold-plated central library. But he left work late, misunderstood me, and arrived on the west corner, a mile away.

So we wander, clueless and together, into a field dotted with clusters of people. As promised, he procures a bottle of rosé, pours two glasses, and asks me about books because he's been paying attention. In between sips and comments, he pauses to stare into the sky, the liquid in his clear plastic cup almost a reflection of the dusky sunset framing his body, the light catching the edges of his dark skin, making him glow, while fireflies flicker in the background. I frame the photo in my mind, imagine it bordered in white on a phone screen.

II. Second Movement

When it gets dark, we leave the park and walk south from where we entered until we come upon an elegant brick mansion just inside the park grounds.

"What's this building?" he asks.

"I don't know," I say. "I've never been over here."

But without speaking—in sync—we agree to trek up the driveway and admire the pillar-lined porch, creep toward the front door to see what it is, this mystery palace tucked into the greenest part of town. A sign reveals it's Litchfield Villa, part of the parks and rec department, but it's more fun to imagine it as the home of an eccentric millionaire flaunting new money by buying an old house and hosting elaborate dinner parties in its fancy halls. We circle around it, peek inside windows.

"Yeah," I say. "I'd live here."

He looks at the villa, looks at me. "Yeah. I'd live here with you."

Then, for fear of being spotted somewhere we shouldn't be, we hustle back down the driveway.

IV. Third Movement

In Park Slope, we slip into the blue Oaxacan restaurant because it's one of the few places open past nine on a Tuesday and I'm doing a terrible job of playing Yelp for him on "my side" of town. They tell us it's BYOB and the kitchen's about to close, so he breaks out the leftover rosé and looks at me to interpret the menu.

"You know Spanish, right?"

"Sort of," I say, surveying unknown dishes and ruminating on the fact that I learned a colonizer's language during my year in Spain.

Over shared entrees while the restaurant empties out, he asks, "So what's your *Frances Ha* story?"

"My *Frances Ha* story?" Then I recall the scene in the movie—the one he remembered was my favorite—where the title character asks her best friend to tell "the story of us" with its far-reaching dreams and unrealistically beautiful futures. So I say, "I'll be a successful book editor who publishes the first children's novel to win the Pulitzer Prize. I'll summer in the South of France, then I'll come home to a three-story brownstone in downtown Brooklyn—which I own—and it will have rooms to spare for all my visiting friends. And yours?"

"Well," he says, leaning back into his seat and making eye contact, "to start, I live in that brownstone with you. . . ."

And it's a line. A total line, but why not? We're all play-acting our way to falling in love. Dating is just an elaborate game of improv, and come on, you'll have more fun if you just "Yes, and" your way along.

V. Coda

The enchantment breaks when we enter the Seventh Ave. station, because the grimy New York City subway is where romance goes to die, where no matter the hour, Cinderella's time is up. He takes the G train north to Williamsburg, I take it south and catch a bus to Flatbush, looking out the window at a row of businesses with their security shutters pulled down, thinking about how easy it is to spend hours with someone and never say their name aloud.

I Love Your Sonnet

Diana Raab

In response to "Sonnet XVII" by Pablo Neruda

Loving you is as easy as my breath
in and out, which sustains me
when we're apart. You might think
you don't know me—but I am the magic
that reaches for you in the night's gloom,
and the shooting star that blasts
its way to your garden's horizon.
Can you feel my gentle hand upon
your shoulder: a hummingbird's
happy flutter? Come lay your head
on my feathery white pillow.
Leave your garden for mine.
I have been waiting long enough.
This is my sonnet for you.

Taking My Own Life

Jessica Rapisarda

Everything ends in late August
in an oceanside tourist town
while making science with a local guy.
He has yellow curls and blue eyes
as blue as the blue giant stars Lambda Scorpii,
which are almost distant beyond math,
maybe one day from Creation,
and the shape of some
perfection smolders there.
Together, we are 100,000
times brighter than the sun.
Light years and light years away.

When we kiss, it's poet suicide.
I lose all interest in the scrawny
swath of crescent moon and any
solemnly cooing night bird
and any night. I am back before
light and dark. I am

heat and possibility.
The dark is just a clean sleep
before the sun explodes
over the ocean, teeming
with vacationers, pasty fathers
in nylon trunks and fat kids
sweating on inflatable floats.

See that girl in the yellow sarong
toeing a sand crab? She's all
alone. But not me.
Goodbye, poetry.

When he skims my thigh,
I erupt into galaxies, expand
past clandestine motel rooms,
fish writhing on their hooks, beyond
the boy sucked out by undertow.
Goodbye, goodbye and goodbye.

Every word I've ever known
becomes a tiny planet, star, meteor,
burning, spitting, pushing out
toward the absolute border,
coda of space, last page.
I am something other
than living—now how do I say it?
Big and getting bigger.

I erupt into galaxies

Girls on TV

Stella Lei

From the Hubble Telescope, galaxies buzz like static, stars pulsing against each other in a luminous haze. A trillion celestial bodies dancing together. Fingers interlocked.

Gemma tells me this as we sit on the couch, watching starlets float through the television's technicolor grain. There's a boy and a girl and they have coiffed hair and swimming pools and he's taking her stargazing because there's a meteor shower and fifteen minutes later they'll kiss under a fire-streaked sky and credits will roll.

I close my eyes and lean against Gemma's shoulder. Pretend the flashing lights are meteors falling. Pretend the matted cotton under me is grass, soft on skin. Pretend there is room for two girls on screen.

When I open my eyes the television has fizzed to black, broadcasting only our blurred reflections. Gemma tosses the remote to the floor, puts her hands on my shoulders, pushes me back. Rusted couch springs pinch bruises on our thighs and we name them Andromeda, after the galaxy, after the girl.

Your Ceiling, Covered in Glow-in-the-Dark Constellations

Rebecca Ruvinsky

Turn off the TV—no,
climb in bed
with me. Cradle me
close, closer. My feet
tangled in your
toes, your breath
fogging up
my neck. There's nothing
to watch, but we'll stare
at the ceiling, count
the stars, and make
wishes on imaginary
meteorites. We are
together, beneath
the night sky. This, too,
is a dream.

Lying on My Back, Looking Up

Rebecca Ruvinsky

I am searching
for you
in the skies,
in the leftovers
of ice
fizzling into memory,
living only
as long as
my eyes are open.
The moon is
unlonely; the night is wide-
open with possibility.
No words, no wishes:
none needed. We brought
this light, we gave
ourselves up
into the gravity
of the moment,
of a single streaking star—
then another.

Bouquet

Rebecca Ruvinsky

When we no longer have flowers,
we will still speak with them.

You will smell roses on my wrists
even when withered bushes

are our remnants of what was.
In the sky, we will see star jasmine,

and as the night passes
back and forth between our lips,

the sugared air will coat our tongues
in remembrances of honeysuckle.

west-northwest

Rebecca Ruvinsky

west-northwest, the wind brings
the fog. the skies are bursting open
above billowing clouds, cracking
like a coconut, spilling its milk
into the universe, birthing a galaxy.
but us, we only know tonight
by its stars, by meteorites slow-rushing
down to Earth in all their serpentine glory.
far beyond us, the icy leftover limbs
of a long-gone comet are turning,
spinning into our gravity, colliding
into the veil—cloaked from our eyes
with a maiden's modesty. we still want
to marry the sky from the stolen glance
of eyes meeting fire before it all spins away
into rushing clouds carefully covering up
the last gap of clear blue night.

In the Sweet By and By

Alice Rogers

A whistle rings out, low and clear through the night.
Rising, falling, eclipsed by another and then another, until the
sounds weave together and the air throbs. Then, silence. The
whine of crickets. A log shifts in the fire. I watch sparks soar
skyward, deep orange against the night sky's blue underbelly.

From the roll next to me, Caleb whispers, "I can't sleep."

Another whistle sounds, wobbly and faraway. I whisper
back, "Neither can I."

Someone is singing now. The air is thick with the smell
of cattle: that warm, animal smell. Their presence bends the
air just as Caleb's does next to me. A huge, stinking mass of
flickering animal life. Drifting on the night air comes a man's
voice, crooning, *I wake in the mornin' afore daylight, and afore I
sleep the moon shines bright . . .*

Caleb, he says, "I keep thinkin' 'bout my momma."

We come from the same town. Came to drive cattle for
the same reason. Probably having the same fears keeping us
both awake, too. Me and Caleb get along like that. We got the
same birthday. My momma always told me we've got the same
fool head too.

"She'll be alright." I clutch at the blanket laid over my
chest, plucking and worrying at the thin edge of it. "Shit.
She'll probably be glad."

That makes him laugh, a soft exhale of breath. I can feel
his eyes on the side of my head but I don't turn to look. The
night sky has me locked in a battle of wills. I figure if I try and
count all those stars I'll fall asleep before long, or at least I'll
be a little wiser about the world if I don't.

Tomorrow is our first real day of driving. So it makes
some sense that we're both awake and staring at the same big
sky. The rest of our outfit are old hands: cowboys so brown
and weatherbeaten they near blend into the scenery. Caleb

and me, we stick out like a pair of sore thumbs, but at least I know I've got driving in my blood: that before me my daddy did it, and before him my granddaddy. Caleb's the first in his family.

On the strip of red Texas ground between our bedrolls lies his hand. I don't need to look to know it. To know that if I unknotted my fingers from my blanket and let my hand fall to the side, I'd find the warm expanse of his waiting for me. The nervous twitch of his fingers. Slowly, I exhale toward the sky. Hear the man sleeping on the other side of me huff and turn over. Still, the song drifts over our camp. Three thousand cattle, the handful of men dwarfed by them. The night watch sing and whistle to let the cattle know the hoofbeats they hear are from friend and not foe. Sure does comfort me too.

"What're *you* thinkin' 'bout?" Caleb's voice splits the quiet night again. He's one of those fellas that will talk himself right up to the edge of sleep. My momma hated the rare nights he'd have to stay with us, for all the talking he did leaking through the thin walls to keep her up along with me. When I don't answer right away, he prompts, "Bill?"

I'm listening to the song. That distant, quiet song. Winding its way through my head in that dreamy way things take on when you're chasing sleep hard. The sound warping and smearing over the distance, over the noise of the prairie and the thousands of shifting, sleeping cattle. I can feel Caleb's attention. As solid as the distant mountains on the horizon; just wobbly, jagged patches of deeper black against the darkness of night.

"Just tryin' to get to sleep," I mumble, though my eyes are still pinned open. Fingers still worrying at my blanket, until I'm sure I'll wake to find it ragged at the edge. I'm thinking about a cigarette, about the tin of tobacco among my belongings. Inside is tucked a tiny brown loaf of the stuff, alongside a thin fold of papers, a few long cook's matches I stole from my momma's box. A photograph of me and Caleb is pasted to the lid: a picture so old he hates to look at it, really. From back before he cut his hair off.

He's talking again. "I should've told my momma where I was headed." Anxiety is a whip crack in his voice.

I say, "She woulda stopped you. Or worse." It'd been bad when he cut his hair. Worse when he started wearing my clothes. "Better for her to read it in a letter once you've got a few hundred miles between you both."

I pick out the Big Dipper in the time it takes for him to reply. A whistle sounds out, clear as a bell. It's the only constellation I know.

"I'm scared she's gonna tell 'em."

'Em, meaning our boss. Meaning the other cowboys. Maybe the cattle themselves, or every other soul we might encounter from here to the trailhead in Kansas. It can't be understated, the way a mother can follow you.

"Nobody's gonna know nothin'," I whisper, with feeling. As much feeling as you can have after a day hauling cattle across a river. I press my tongue against a split in my lip; long and sore, right down the middle. It tastes tangy, like the memory of the blood. "Far as they know you're just a fella lookin' to drive cattle. No reason for them to think otherwise."

Silence. I close my eyes. Caleb's hand still lies between us. His eyes still needle into the side of my head. It's funny, the things that keep us awake. Me, I can't get there because I want it too bad. Sleep's like a flighty girl: as soon as you let it know you want it, it disappears. So here I am. Thinking about how tired I'm gonna be when me and Caleb are called up for our night watch. How tired I'm gonna be for our first full day driving. About how I better not get nothing wrong, with all this cattle driving blood in my veins.

Caleb, well. Maybe if he laid there and counted as many stars as I have, he'd realize just how tiny he is in this world. Too tiny for God to make any trouble for him.

I add, "What's important is you're here. The hardest part's done."

We'd left before dawn to catch up with the outfit; Caleb riding behind me, his arms clutched around my waist. The two of us silent, as if by speaking we'd somehow summon his momma, or my parents; a search party good at seeking out wayward girls. With us we carried all we needed and little more. Some food I filched from the pantry, bound up in cheesecloth. A canteen, my tobacco tin, a set of my clothes that Caleb changed into as soon as we were far enough from home to feel comfortable stopping. His nightdress he balled up and tossed as far as he could throw it, and when that wasn't far enough, he ran after it and stepped on it, trod it into the red sand and jumped on it. I watched from afar, smoking.

When we got back on the horse, Caleb put his face against my nape and stayed there like that. His hot breath fogging the hollow behind my ear. Then the sun rose, flooding into the valley and stirring away that grainy gray air that comes with dawn. An hour later we were getting signed on for a three-hundred-mile trip to Kansas.

The prairie in summertime usually smells hot and sweet. All I can smell in this starlit, midnight moment is cattle and baked dirt. I take a great lungful of it in, and still my fingers in their nervous plucking. The singer has stopped. Rhythmic, scattered whistles have replaced his song.

At my side, Caleb says, "You really think that was the hardest part?"

No, I think, but I don't say it. Instead, I roll my head to the side and finally meet the eyes that have been prickling at me all night. Caleb's face is a mess of shadows, pooling under his lip, in the curve of his cheek, the hollow of his temple. His thick blond hair like a thatch on his head. He's made of stern stuff, in his own way. But still, I lie. I murmur, "Yeah, that was the worst of it."

A man a few rolls down from us is snoring. Not awful. Not like the kinda raspy snores I hear from my parents' room at home. Just soft, snuffling sounds. Enough to make me drowsy; drowsier than I'd got counting those damn stars anyway. I feel my eyes start to droop. Caleb has turned away, seems to be tracing the cobalt underbelly of the sky just as I'd been. I wanna say to him, *you ain't gonna get nothin' from that*, but my tongue is too heavy to lift. All I can do is stare at his profile and extend my hand into that strip of Texas between our beds.

Sure enough, I find his hand there. Waiting for me like he knew it was just a matter of time before I sought it out. Our knuckles touch, our fingers curl together. His palm is damp and warm. Pulse thrumming when I push my fingertips to his wrist.

Out in the night, someone is singing again. His voice drifting over the plains, a perfect cattle call: sweet and sad, blue as the night sky.

Conflagrant

Sher Ting

The lake rises and falls in a storm of gravity,
tethered to the night's wandering face.

The moon is a curved wishbone in the sky, split
into light and darkness the way all dreams are.

You asked me if I'd ever believe that fireflies
are repositories for our dreams, waiting on

the sprigs of sycamore for the first light of a
sleep-kilned reverie, watching a constellation

of flame-kissed embers drift into the night sky before
coming to rest in their belly, hungry for a home.

You told me how summers as an adult are different
from summers as a child, the way silver rusts in a glare

of sunlight, wonder breaks in the light of growth,
the years have shaped your body into a fleshed quilt-work

of scars and phantom bruises, sleepless nights hollowing
themselves into your chest, and your mind still yearns for the ghosts

of fireflies.

Today,
it chases them still.

Pinpricks

Sarah Ernestine

Fireflies hover above my head
like paper lanterns that forgot to rise,
weaving through cooling air,
following an invisible thread.

The smell of crackling logs
clings to my hair
like perfume, masking
the tall pines at my back.

The muscles in my legs hum
like an electric pulse as rays of sunlight
fade between trunks, seeing how far
they can run before bending beyond the horizon.

The smoke dances on the breeze
like flowing ribbons on a maypole,
tugging the remaining leaves from their branches
to cloak the ground below.

As I move nearer to the fire,
I hear the repetitive call of a songbird somewhere
deep in the forest, offering her song like a lullaby
as the day begins to fade into a memory.

One by one, the stars poke holes
into the blanket of dark sky;
their silent hellos flickering to
the lightning bugs still hanging above my head.

The Archive

Sarah Ernestine

I fell in love with
a woman
who collects sea glass
in a jam jar.

When others train their eyes
to the pitching waves,
she looks down—
bare feet and smooth stones.

Her fingers harvest
colored, weather-worn
shards of stars
from the Earth.

She holds them to the sky—
the sun's light
reminding them how it felt
to glint in velvet heavens.

Champagne bottles and car lights—
fractured joy, brittle pain.
Salted air weaves tendrils of my hair
and reminds me to inhale.

A fragment of my heart
will remain there forever—
nestled among shattered moments
long after my name becomes an echo.

Honey-
(comb)

Taylor Wyna Stewart

Honeycomb, that's what I remember about June. That crisp taste, that bucolic sweetness from stall number four at Pepper Place Market. It was the time for spilled beer on picnic tables, gorging on blackberries in Ms. Beck's backyard, it was the time for coconut-scented sunscreen, and listening to Young the Giant. Sunhats, overalls, cheap flip-flops that crackle on the sidewalks, our skips from the market like little poems fetched from dusk. There was nothing more I dreamed of than cool nights on our porch whispering of constellations and what blessings mother moon would send us.

You'd take a book from my shelf, flip through it until you found page 42, and read that page whether it was verse or story, or a chapter on how to properly fix a leaky faucet. It was like Shakespeare, standing tall and holding the treasured honeycomb like poor Yorick's skull. June was the time for happiness, and you.

There's a growling quiet now, which I like, it's a soft murmur when the inky silk sky is cloudless and I have the chance to spy all the blue, red, and white stars I want—a few planets here and there. Autumns and winters and all kinds of sweltering Julys have come and gone and yet I remember your stories better than my own. Summer's come again, they say, with its sweat and tears and fears of what will come round in the fall.

I figured you'd be here, your voice breathes on my porch. I try not to gasp but even in this light you are almost fairer than a ghost. Look at you now in that collared top, you smell like jet lag and complimentary pretzels. They've made you crop your hair so it stays in line. You look like a real professional now. They say it when your mother talks about that job of yours, he's a *re-uhl* professional now, they say it—just like that—drawing out that word like one of our honeycombs.

It's my house, I say, looking back down at my book, *where else I'd be?* There's a creak on that bottom step I know well, like a faint moan. I let my eyes flicker, seeing your bent knee—it's your loafer that's causing that sound. As if being closer will make me forget. I want to shout, I want to scream, why should I pay any attention to you when you hardly think of me at all. *You should have called*, I say, swallowing. Not that it woulda made a difference.

Soon you're close, your index finger trailing down the side of my cheek. It's so cool against this night, these fairy-tale stars blinking their light in my yard. *I know you like a surprise*, you whisper. It hurts to look, it hurts to remember the sound of a rolling suitcase and the smell of burned espresso beans at the airport. *Can we go for a walk?* It's the first time your voice has ever imitated softness—the first time you've ever asked me for permission.

Are those new glasses? I blink, reaching up to brush the stray curl on your temple. For some reason I stand up and let you take my hand. There's about a half dozen lizards snaking up my drainpipe and across the garage door. *You gotta do something about that*, you say, eyeing one of the lime-green ones.

They don't bother me. I shrug, letting my palm fit inside yours just like it used to. Why am I doing this, why do I let you do this? Am I nostalgic or is it some midsummer spell cast on me like some unsuspecting tragedy? There are no questions that pass from my mouth or yours, because there are no questions. We have nosy friends and even nosier relatives who pass our movements to each other. I know you had someone at that school of yours, some Oregonian with a warm smile who took you to see all those whales you've dreamed of. I wonder, could you see Cetus in the sky that night? Did the waves crash and swirl and foam until that kiss drowned you to the bottom of that underworld you built? I feel like you want me to bring you back here only to turn and see your spirit shift and leave our home again.

On this bruised asphalt my sneakers dodge potholes, all the while your strong hand keeps me steady. There's nothing like the sky after twilight, and I think back to all those June berries, the seasonal cheeses the Piggly Wiggly carried, and scrumptious springtime nectar. *I said I'd be back, my term is up now,* you tell me in that folksy tune. The neighborhood lights have dimmed even though I can tell one has stayed on long enough just to see who's walking around after dark.

There is power in this truth, a cool and breezy harvest you've brought home to me. I spy your freckles, a new constellation that only comes this time of year. I don't think I can anymore, is your truth, a promise you mean to keep by coming back to this town. It's your voice that draws me back. Why do I let it, knowing that June has to end.

How is it, I want to ask, that after all these years, all these seasons—you still taste like honeycomb?

The Night's Stars

Natalie Marino

An early summer night.

We stare at stars and you hold me
on the balcony's edge.

The air around us is black
and we are still

like babies the moment before birth
and I know

I can leave you in the morning.
We drink a glass

of sparkling white wine and your hand
is on my shoulder.

Now I know love like I know the sky.

Firefly Songs

Natalie Marino

My husband's heart
is a bowl of red tulips.
Love is eating color,
despite the universe.

I cry counting
the dying fireflies
inside a closed jar.
When we watch

the open sky
with a tin telescope,
we laugh at not seeing
the same bright stars.

Evanescence

Natalie Marino

A summer evening
after garden hose
waterfall delights—

the afternoon
was a bright blue balloon,
now the sky turns violet.

An early moon shines silver,
making the grass
a wild sea,

and my father points out
the honking geese
flying home.

He lets them go
like we let go of time.
My child eyes see

truth tellers dancing naked
to their own joy songs
under stars being born.

Summer Starlight

Natalie Marino

In a photograph taken in 1911
my six-year-old grandmother
holds hope in her eyes.

I see the same dreams
in my daughters.

The stems of surprise
lilies grow at night
under honey starlight

while I watch time falling
through my fingers.

I can still hold love
inside my summer
marmalade jar.

Going Home

Natalie Marino

On August nights when the air
is as thick as molasses,

orange lamplight stars show me the way
to pick up

the dust left from memories.
My children count

raindrops and draw smiles on windows.
I already ate the blue eternity

and silver lines in clouds,
and now

my sticky hands hold
on to the sky.

We go home with morning
butterflies.

Should We Stay Up Late on Independence Day

Matthew Miller

Shriveled July grass. Sparklers crack in erratic
spasms. Twilight above us rumbles and whines,
out of breath, the dizziness of freedom in its eyes.
How many days burst over us before we realize
it's too late, it must be bedtime—the kids are cranky,
deerflies bite, dry strands snag in a hair tie. Scattered shells.
A skyrocket that didn't ignite. We are anxious with possibility,
nightswimming. We should splash in before sleep, dive
into shadows together. We know we are tired, but the cicadas rise,
vibrating like the laughter of a child. Above us,
clouds slide past the moon, fireflies collide
with their reflections on the water. Our arms are quiet,
and we know we are right to watch our children
smile, faces slick with the ripples of light
as summer heat subsides, stars stretch toward each other,
and the hours grow full and wide.

In the Light of Wonder

Jakky Bankong-Obi

For Dotuchowo

Side by side. We watch an orange sun   defunct the sky &
the half-moon shimmer of mid-August unveil   the gloaming.
How the future abuts the past & all present exigencies fade.
& memory becomes all but night's inky overcast   -   where
only the brightest fragments shine   -   like stars punctuating
the dark. I know this moment will be ours forever.   *The beauty
of shared memories is that they hold us together.*
Mother to son, we bait the telescope pending the stars' stellar preen.
Your hand in mine, a weight I will carry forever & pray this light
never quits your eyes & the worth of all expectations   shine in
the luminous aspects of your face,   a mirror::a door
I open & suddenly   a reachable miracle;   joy.
Your laughter like a shooting star, unfettered across all our skies.
& it grows & grows so it seems the night's prized constellations,
which were at first impossible   &   removed
now spotlight here. as though an aperture has somehow unfolded
this ordinary life into wonder.

constellations //.

Holly Ruskin

i lay the
velvet drape
of night over
you and pull
stars down
to place in
your eyes
now plucked
and heavy
made ready
for rest and
your body
curls tightly
into mine

our edges
are crested
by moonlit
sea foam
as waves
of sleep
lap gently
at our feet
while your
breath works
to lull me
into slumber

and as you
drift away
it's these nights
spent making light
of constellations
that I'll remember
long after you
are grown and
i go to
bed

alone

pull stars down
to place in your eyes

The Summer Before I Turn Fifty

Kristin Van Tassel

---

along Glimmerglass camping lake, fireflies blink against
night's black starprickle stretch. One tent site over, church

women with braids lean into slantminor harmony, their circle
a tent-framed silhouette. East by northeast, finger inlets washed

in rising sun—light trickles between fir and pine, bright green
mosslace aglow like bioluminescent fish airborne. I swing round

southwest toward home to find space enough for ribclouds lining
the sky—diving into the horizon of prairie's wideyawn. When I

trace my body's signature across last summer's wind, I touch a
stillwarm single milk pearl, fifteen years since I last nursed, its

luster a beacon of wonder.

it must be nice not to believe in god

Joyce Liu

no.
it's lonely.

where do you find the sacred?
in mother's hands,
in paper trains and dirty glasses,
in icy metal against summer legs,
listening to the music play from your broken earbuds
and staring at the sky,
waiting for something to happen,
waiting for someone you know will never come for you.

our father who art in heaven
named me after happiness and art.
xin
like heart.
xin
like new.
xin like the sound of a blade unsheathing,
like the sword in my last name,
hanging in the wings,
waiting.
nobody knows who we are waiting for,
but we do it anyway,
we of the patio swings and the plastic suburban slides.
god, i'm sorry the art isn't happy.
i have nothing greater to put my trust in,
no cosmic parent;
i orphaned myself a decade ago and i haven't seen you since.

---

who will forgive me for my unforgiveables?
who will gift me absolution for everything i've done?
when i'm dying,
when i'm sitting here alone, with nobody to answer to
except myself and whoever sits between stars,
who will weigh my heart and tell me i was enough?
i need someone to sit next to me on the swings.
i need them to say, quietly, without looking at me,
that i can put it down.
i have nobody to kneel for anymore.
no ghosts,
no god,
no graves,
our ruthless stars—

silent.

i am waiting for someone to come back for me.
i am still the lost child in the walmart magazine aisle
but it's past closing hours and nobody is looking.
i am sitting here, asking the sky if you've forgotten me in the store,
and waiting a lifetime for it to blink back.

staring at the sky

waiting for something to happen,
waiting for someone you know
will never come for you

The
Desecrated
Wood

Mallory Pearson

don't ask me if you don't want to hear that it was like the car had run out of gas, and the rain was a current down the cul-de-sac, and the summer was a woman with her hair pulled back, and the cicadas were humming to each other just to get the vibration out, and the pool was sputtering through its drying mouth, and the billboards called out about loving your sins, and my body became a blooming thing like the leaves of a revived ash tree, and it was on fire, and it was ash again, eventually.

you really want to know? it was hotter than hell and i hated the suffocating air only slightly more than the bad dreams. i missed the weight of virginia humidity. an indiana storm was a lot like living in a fishbowl. kyle smoked in the middle of the road, kelly read in her armchair, and the bullfrog was a sound that turned my bird body into a metronome.

i saw things that weren't there, dark blots that i didn't care to consider much. kyle said annie was a lesbian and now maybe she isn't, and he looked at me when he said it. kelly said there was a man who used to scare her and we both knew he still was, somewhere across the world, hurting her without saying it.

we didn't want to think about it so we walked the cornfields, catching lightning bugs, chewing clover, pretending to be bigger than we were. i took a shower kneeling in the bathtub and the stairs creaked. kyle went out to smoke again, kelly's thick lock turned, safe for the night, and we all felt a little haunted in the big dark air. i read their cards. i told them that they're tired. i told them to open themselves up and say that they're tired.

only kelly knew what that indiana was like for me. the moon was a big orange womanly thing over the cornfields, light all snatched away for the evening and saved in a jar. over the hill, someone had a brush fire going, and every bird that nested in the rusting old ford was crooning for touch. in the end, my body remembered two things: grief and stars. the forsythia was a house for my younger self and the graves of dogs. kelly texted me from ohio where she was a woman again, no binds, and i was on my side in a child's bed, begging for sleep.

my body remembered two things:

grief

and stars

Instead of Sleeping

Mallory Pearson

i went out to the fields. the middle of the night, those tense little touches, all the swaying and singing made the barn doors open. it was my birthday. we swam all night, the sky chocolate orange against the illuminated blue of the pool. just being able to breathe the untouched air. everywhere the forsythia, like the constant stretch of a brush fire, expanding out across the farmland. i didn't know quite what i was or where i wanted to go.

we left trampled buttercups where the ground knew no grass. wasn't it sweet, to hold the feeling up to your chin and see the reflection? then the rain came down in torrents. we slept in your childhood bedroom. in the middle of the night, the floorboards creaked, and all the families on church street felt a little uneasy. the midday sun was unbearably bright, and i remembered that i wasn't quite as steady on my feet as i liked to think. it was a bad habit i formed when i was younger. having little to no luck around the scale, or the river, or the bend of her knee.

i took a break from being a know-it-all. i went back home for a little while. everyone said *don't rush into it* and instead i just fucking ran. the storm drain was just a prop for the river styx and i cut my foot open on the rocks, blood offering. i wanted something more significant. i planted an apple tree. the apples were always rotten little things. i was never really soft enough to wear the dress or hard enough to take it off. always a misshapen mouth in an ageless body, waiting for instruction.

virginia is pink all over. a place made for crows and the like.

it all felt wrong so i took to the mountains on an endless road. the sound of the wind was just wings around me. she was afraid of hawks so i talked about them more. usually i would have been sick at the thought of the diner, but i got my bearings.

in the end, it didn't matter if i was a woman or a girl. i chose to thunder-walk. my body had mass and sound. i went tiptoeing and the house was groaning and i had a dream where i was strong enough to carry you over my shoulder and it meant nothing after waking, in the end. i miss who i was in the last skin and now i'm unknowable, unrecognized, unnamed and rotting in the woods behind some overgrown fence.

it would be easier to move home if i knew where that was, if i wasn't always missing something else. if the blinking bullets of light overhead would just wink out for once.

if the blinking bullets of light over-
head would just wink out for once

A Dirt-Red Star Shaped Like Mars

Mallory Pearson

bonfire before the sun sets. the cicadas aren't awake
yet. i wait for them by the back door,
letting the sugar burn in the pan. good night
to the sweet tea, sweet peas, peonies body-like
in the breeze. it is so stupidly easy to be asleep.
i ask myself questions like
are you looking at me? do you think about
having hurt me, up and restless
beneath a prairie of white sheets?
the silos fall, towers of grain, and we mourn
like they are tombstones for giants of wheat,
leaning forlorn into evenings
where the sun yawns across an overgrown lawn.
while holding your arm, i dreamt of your cheek.
while holding your cheek, i dreamt of your arm.
exhausted from all the tossing and turning.
wasting away on a cot set up for spare nights.
nesting behavior, a lot like knowing
i'll love the most charismatic girl in the room
as long as she touches my hand.
similar to a bird in the sense
that i know my patterns and i like the familiar.
in candlelit dark i sit in the tub and thumb out
methods of change, pinch fat here and there, taste acid.
who was that girl when she refused to eat?
only me. only ever me.

painting

Aral L.

it is a lucky thing
if a summer night holds a mouthful of stars
wide enough to fit under,
wide enough to look up at.
it is a lucky thing
to have a neck that bends backward
and lets you face something
other than the ground.
and if in a painting
you are nothing more than a smudge,
a little bit of dark
to keep you from blending into the grass,
then at least you are something.
at least someone has painted you.

Buoyancy

Emily L. Pate

Blue sky breaks into silver and rain
falls all in a rush on the abandoned
Boy Scouts camp, onto lake and evergreens
and broken picnic tables, more splinter
than shape even before storm paints all
to blur and color, baring the world close
to the bone. Memory is no easy thing
to drown, but the lake jumps and ripples closer
to itself, fills banks until loneliness forgets
what it was and swims.

Sheltering California

Emily L. Pate

Originally published in The Rising Phoenix Review *in January 2021*

California ushers me in again, my childhood state
an envelope of blue sky folding over. Every evening,
I take the dog through the open spaces tucked behind
suburbia, riding my bike on deer trails, grass hip-high.
I've ridden these trails so often the dirt remembers
the shape of my tires like I remember the way my brother walks,
so that two years ago, when illness leaned his face
unrecognizable, I still knew him across a crowded airport,
just by the way he moved. These California hills love flowers:
the delicate orange cup of a poppy, the thin reaching
of yellow mustard flower, little purple blossoms close
to the ground. The dog runs beside me, grass folding him in
as he startles a turkey into a plum tree. Fishline-thin telephone
wires bend between hills round as sleeping hips and heads
and shoulders, ready to roll over into the California earthquake
we're long overdue on. Cows cluster in oak tree shadows,
stick-legged babies heart-centered, and a breeze carries
the hay-heavy smell of horses. Grass bows under wind, bends
to the summer sky, and I sway with it. There is no purer blue
than what arcs over California, pouring between the branches
of oak trees, catching threads on barbed wire fences.
Once, my cousin lay in the backyard sun so long a vulture
started silent circling the blue above her, singing hunger through
the heat. So much in this life is singing, air whistling past
as I pedal an incline, hawks screaming overhead. Wings are
always circling in California, something always cutting this sky.

The Speed of Things

Thomas J. Misuraca

As Sean rode in the comfort of Joel's car, he watched the sun slowly set over the Pacific Ocean. He couldn't believe he'd only known this man for a week. Yet, he felt as comfortable with him as with people he'd known his entire life.

They held hands as Sean took in the beautiful landscape.

He didn't want this moment to end.

Joel stepped on the gas. The sun was setting too quickly. The orange sphere was vanishing from the horizon; the sky turning a gradient of dark blue to purple.

He swerved his BMW into the parking lot of Zuma Beach. Thankfully there was a parking spot close to the stairs.

Once Joel parked the car, Sean leaned in to give him a quick peck on the cheek.

Sean must have misunderstood Joel's intentions. They weren't stopping for a make-out session. They had to get to the beach.

"Let's go," Joel playfully urged as he pulled away from Sean's lips. He got out of the car, hoping Sean would quickly follow.

Sean crossed his arms over his chest. The beach air was chilly, and he wore only a T-shirt. Joel opened the trunk of his car and pulled out two sweaters. He handed one to Sean.

"I brought an extra," he told Sean. "Just in case."

Sean thought that was the most romantic thing ever.

Arm in arm they slowly made their way to the beach.

Joel had thought his romance days were over. He had given up going to bars, searching personal ads, and looking for quickies on hookup apps. He'd accepted the fact that he'd be spending the rest of his days alone.

Then he met Sean in line at the DMV. Joel was complaining about the preposterous wait. Sean responded with funny observations of the people around him:

"That guy who failed the vision test must be a has-been actor who never was. He refuses to wear glasses because he thinks he can still be cast as a cool teen."

"Oh honey, no matter how much makeup you put on before you take your photo, it's going to look like crap."

"That guy at the end of the line is reading *War and Peace.* What's he going to do when he finishes?"

A DMV visit had never passed so quickly.

Sean joked that while most of his friends met online, he and Joel met in line. At the DMV of all places. Sean hoped that cute guy in line with him would still be there after he concluded his visit. But, damn, there were so many steps to renew his license. Each seemed to take forever.

As luck would have it, they ended up in line for their photos at the same time.

"How's my hair?" Sean asked Joel.

"Perfect," Joel replied with a killer smile.

Sean flashed his business card and handed it to Joel.

"Call me the next time you're waiting in line and need a good laugh," Sean told him.

Joel studied Sean's card. It was colorful and eye-catching. The guy was clearly in business for himself. As Joel placed it in his wallet, he removed one of his boring-in-comparison corporate cards and handed it to Sean. Without looking at it, Sean slipped the card into his back pocket. A moment later, Sean was summoned to take his picture.

That night, Joel paced around his house. He wanted to call Sean, but it was too soon. He had to wait three days, right? Would the night after tomorrow be a good length of time? How would he keep occupied until then?

Suddenly, his phone rang.

"I couldn't wait to call you," Sean blurted into his phone the moment Joel picked up. He warned himself not to babble like an idiot. "How'd your picture come out?"

"Think Freddy and Jason had a baby with a receding hairline," Joel told him.

"Weren't they both bald?"

"Yeah! Lucky them."

Sean laughed. "I look like I'm drunk, stoned, and just went ten rounds with The Rock."

From there, their conversation rolled on like a freight train.

When Sean hung up, he was surprised that two hours had passed.

Joel stared at the time stamp on his phone. Two hours? He never talked on the phone that long. It was past the time he usually started getting ready for bed.

As he washed up and brushed his teeth, he chuckled, remembering Sean telling him how he found a fingernail in a pot of coffee at one of the offices where he did temp work.

"Finding nine-finger Betty was a cinch," Sean told him. It was the stupidest thing, but Joel got a big kick out of it.

It took Joel longer than usual to fall asleep because he was anxious and excited about the date they planned for Saturday night.

Sean feared Saturday would never arrive. He had two days of work and one day of figuring out how to pass the time before he got to see Joel again. The boring office temp job dragged. Every time he looked at the clock, it was earlier than he thought it was.

He sat at home Friday night, cursing himself for not making the date that night. Twenty-four hours had never passed so slowly.

Joel's week was a whirlwind. He had an impossible amount of projects to finish. In order not to come into work on Saturday, he worked late Friday night. He was tempted to call Sean from his office but didn't want to look desperate.

He woke up early Saturday morning to get started on his housework and errands. There was no way he'd get them all done before he had to start getting ready for his date.

A date! Joel still couldn't believe it.

Though dinner at seven o'clock was far too late. By the time they got seated and ordered, the food wouldn't arrive until eight o'clock.

Sean thought seven o'clock was a little too early for dinner, but he was so anxious to see Joel, he got to the restaurant fifteen minutes early.

Joel had picked the place and made the reservations. When Sean arrived, he feared this dinner would set his budget back a couple of weeks.

After a long wait, Sean glanced at his phone. It was five minutes past seven. Joel wasn't there yet. The guy must have gotten cold feet.

Much to Sean's relief, Joel showed up moments later.

"Been waiting long?" he asked Sean.

"No," Sean lied.

When they got to their table, Joel ordered a bottle of sparkling wine. Sean was scared to look at the price on the wine list.

They chatted while sipping wine and munching on bread, constantly sending the waiter away because they never got around to looking at the menu.

Joel worried they'd never get to eat. It was almost eight o'clock, and though he was immensely enjoying Sean's company, his stomach was growling. By this time, the restaurant would begin running out of items.

Still, they talked on and on and on.

Sean was surprised and relieved when Joel paid the bill. Sean offered his credit card, but Joel refused it.

"You'll get the next one," Joel told him.

"Hope you like Denny's," Sean half-joked.

"I'd enjoy any place with you for company."

Was Joel being intentionally goofy? Not that it mattered, it made Sean giddy to hear somebody say something so nice about him.

Joel had valeted while Sean had parked a few streets over.

"I'll drive you," Joel suggested. Sean didn't object.

They ended up sitting and talking in Joel's car until past midnight. Their conversations evolved into a kissing session. It started with sweet little pecks but quickly escalated into passionate embraces. Sean wanted to take this guy home and have marathon sex.

Joel hadn't stayed out past midnight in years. He dreaded the next morning. Even though it was Sunday, his body clock would automatically wake him early. He'd be fatigued while finishing his errands. He hoped to schedule a catnap.

It was worth it to share romantic kisses with a sweet guy. As of late, kisses were just a gateway to getting naked. Joel was happy taking things slow with Sean.

Maybe this was more than a flash in the pan romance.

Sean realized he'd never had lunch with a guy the day after a date, unless they'd spent the night together. But there he was, having lunch with Joel on Sunday.

It took a long time and all his willpower for Sean to leave Joel's car. He never ended a date with somebody he liked without getting naked. Not getting it made him want it more.

He barely slept that night. He couldn't get Joel out of his mind. He thought it was too early to call him on a Sunday morning to thank him for dinner, but Joel sounded awake and refreshed.

"It was a great first date," Sean said. Then panicked. What if this guy didn't think it was a date? No, that make-out and groping session at the end assured him it was.

"Yeah." Joel sounded as if he were giggling.

"But we forgot to do the one thing that defines a good first date," Sean said.

"Well . . . I thought, maybe we should wait—"

"We didn't plan a second date!" Sean blurted out to halt Joel's discomfort.

"Oh." Joel sounded pleasantly surprised. "When would you like to go out again?"

"I'm free tonight!"

"Oh?"

Sean silently palmed his skull. He was going to scare this guy off by being too anxious.

"How about a late lunch?" Joel asked.

Hours later, they were eating sushi and continuing their nonstop conversation.

Again, Joel refused to take any money from Sean.

Joel did his best to focus on Sean's company, and not the millions of things he had to do before Monday.

Lunch turned into shopping. Joel hoped he could check a few items off of his mental to-do list, but they visited mostly novelty shops.

"Nobody's ever bought me a teddy bear before," Sean told him as they left a toy shop.

"Never?" Joel was surprised.

"Got a stuffed monkey once, but never a classic teddy. I'll name him JoJo, after you."

Joel tried not to picture the bear ripped to shreds after their relationship ended.

"Dinner?" Sean suggested.

Joel surprised himself by agreeing. He usually spent Sunday nights at home watching *60 Minutes* and *The Simpsons* while indulging in his weekly allowance of pasta.

After dinner, the car make-out sessions continued.

As much as he hated to do it, Joel told Sean: "I have to work tomorrow."

It didn't feel like Sunday night. The weekend flew by in a flash. Granted, Sean didn't have work lined up that week, so he could sleep in if he wanted. But when Joel said, "I have to work tomorrow," Sean knew it wasn't fun waking up on a Monday morning after a weekend of fun.

"You can't leave until we plan our next date," Sean teased.

"Wednesday?" Joel asked.

Midweek seemed decades away.

"Sure," Sean replied excitedly.

"We could head to the beach," Joel suggested.

"I'd like that. What time?"

"Let's say seven o'clock. Gives me enough time to get home and freshen up."

"Okay."

"I can pick you up, if you want," Joel said.

Sean smiled. He wanted.

Joel dreaded looking at his phone on Monday and Tuesday. He had an irrational fear that Sean would cancel Wednesday night. This was their third date, and the fourth time they'd be together. Joel hadn't spent this much time with another man in ages.

He almost had a heart attack when he saw a text pop up from Sean on Tuesday afternoon. It read: "Confirming our 7:00 Wednesday night date. Can't wait!"

Joel did the math in his head, and realized, if he rushed, he could be done with work, freshened up, and at Sean's by six-thirty.

Joel texted back: "Could pick you up at 6:30 if that's better."

Instantly, Sean replied: "Perfect."

Sean's apartment had never been so clean. He focused on cleaning to fill the three days before he saw Joel again. He wanted to call him every afternoon and night, but it sounded like the guy had a stressful job, and he didn't want to bother him. A quick confirmation text was a safe bet. Sean didn't think he'd hear back from him, but to his surprise, he later got a text asking to start the date earlier.

Still, it felt like an eternity before he saw Joel's car pull up in front of his building. Sean had been waiting outside for ten minutes.

Joel pulled Sean toward the beach. He couldn't remember the last time he came to the beach to watch the summer sunset. He'd spent the past five years focusing on his job, neglecting his social and dating life. Seasons flew by. One minute it was the long days of July, the next the sun was setting at four-thirty.

They sat and snuggled on the sand.

It was finally feeling like summer to Sean. Slow, warm days and long, active nights. Memorial Day was a distant memory, Labor Day far in the future. Sean savored these precious moments with Joel.

One by one, the stars appeared in the sky.

Joel and Sean walked the length of the beach and back again, their arms wrapped around each other. Both dreaded the inevitable end to this date. And the long wait until they saw each other again. Both hoped for a summer, and possibly lifetime, filled with long, slow nights that would pass in a flash.

Honey-mooners

Victoria Schofield Dobbs

ONE.
The ad reads *escape the crowds*
so we book a starship without another thought,
wanting to explore space, to float
the unending shimmering sea
of the Milky Way, counting comets overhead.

Then we take the sky rail, the cosmic interstate,
from Earth to Europa for a quick cruise
within its icy shell, our wetsuits packed
for windsurfing or snorkeling. We visit
sugar-sand beaches, try the local cuisine:
a puffed cloud of yeast, a translucent feast
from a new wave chef.

Five-star accommodations,
light jazz, wool blankets,
cuddled in a private igloo
burning for warmth. Its walls melt
then refreeze as the sun slips away.

TWO.
I had forgotten what it was like to lie
in the dark, stare at the stars, and dream.

The Starfish Is Also a Star

Ismim Putera

The stars fall like snowy rain
        one or two land
        on our hands—
        sprawled like hungry starfishes
        staining the river golden green

Starfishes are born from the stars
        when they blinked for too long
        and eventually detached
        into icy comets
        granting wishes bloomed in dreams

Row faster! The starfishes are blooming
        catch the starfishes—
        you are terribly good at it
        the river: pink, then purple, then azure
        the water swirls into rainbow vortices

Don't kiss them yet—
        their spongy limbs
        are sour and bitter
        kiss me, first, as always—
        my coral lips taste like starfishes too

The starfishes glitter into small stars
        shimmering in the river of time
        let them blink and blink and blink
        watching us bathe
        in this Milky Way

that sea, that salvation

Madison Zehmer

Originally published in Milly Magazine

---

i. then

sick and seabound / we mined our bodies for stars / piled them up one by one until soul remnants ached alone / separated from flesh //

a sort of self-inscribed punishment / we buried ourselves beneath sinking ships / let anchors spear us in two / our soulstars cleaved from each other / swirling down toward shifting sand //

we pressed lips of salt into prayer / let words filling our bellies rot in the emptiness //

some starving thing desired us / and we longed for it / that slow feeling of nothingness / our food and our flesh //

I was one of these girls / or I wanted to be / cast out to the ocean to drown / cast out by my own doing / my own sickness / my own desire / to fall apart / to fall asleep //

so I hung in a netherworld between consciousness / dead and breathing / alive / choking / something in between //

and then / when I desired to become more human than siren / I woke up / slowly / grabbed an anchor to steady me / let it bring me back to earth //

---

ii. now

the world turns / slow and solid /and I mine the sky for stars
/ and I leave my body alone //

a starving thing desires me / but I do not desire it anymore /
the heartache of losing oneself already with me //

how does one unite soul and stars and flesh? //

I let my skin grow when it wants / let breath escape through
my ribs / and mingle with air / let sky guide me home / rather
than soil //

it still rains / and I am still seabound / but I am no longer sick
/ and I no longer want to be //

the salt of air as sweet as the salt of sea //

let sky guide me home

Sojourners

Anna Caldwell

After the engines cut out, we drifted for days on the high ice. We listened to the unfamiliar language of our surroundings, the creaking moans and whistles and gunshot-cracks of the stark white shelves. Guillemots screeched and huddled against sheer cliffs. The waves were an incessant slap against the hull.

Most of those on board stayed below, but some of us wandered out on deck, maybe searching for anything that could help, maybe just wanting to die with our faces to the open sky. A strange, wordless camaraderie started to form between those of us who remained outside.

It became an endless task to stave off hunger and boredom. I watched the sea and the sky, breathed in the salt spray, slept between coils of rope in the milk half-light of near constant dawn. One day, just after sunrise, I woke to someone shaking my shoulder gently. I knew her face—dark, narrow eyes and thick brows, above the scarf covering her mouth—but not her name or voice. When she spoke, it was low and deeply musical.

"Look," she said, and pointed toward something I couldn't see.

I dragged myself up and staggered to the starboard side of the ship. While I slept, we'd covered some distance, and now we drifted past a shore of jagged stones. A little way up this beach, mountains rose, solid and dark. They gathered breaths of cloud about their peaks. We were fast approaching the midnight sun, but at this hour the light was dim enough that I could see a freckling of faint stars across the sky behind them.

At the nearest summit, where the woman's shaking hand pointed, something else shimmered.

I tilted my head to look at it. At certain angles in this light, there was a doorway. It glinted cerulean like the water of warmer seas and, as we watched, it waxed bright and then waned, becoming indistinct again.

It was with a jolt of surprise I realized others had joined us.

"What is it?" The man who had spoken was a mountain himself, tall and bearded, with a voice like flint striking.

"A way out, maybe," the woman said. "At the very least, a curiosity worth investigating."

Maps were produced, our approximate location pinpointed. Still we drifted. I watched the stone beach and the shimmering doorway, my bare hand pressed to the railing like the sharp cold would tether me to reality. The others argued.

"There is no such island." Sparks flew from a grindstone voice. He towered over her, but she held his gaze and kept her own voice level.

"There is nothing at all," she said. "Soon we'll reach the ice sheet. What then?"

"We try radio communication again. We search for trappers, settlements. We don't chase after mirages."

"You mean we carry on drifting, and slowly we die. Do what you like. I'm taking the raft, whether anyone else comes or not."

"I'll go," I said. I hadn't spoken in days; my voice was rough and quiet, but they all looked at me. The man laughed.

We didn't try to convince them to join us.

Our journey was short, the water choppier than I had expected. Neither of us spoke. I examined my new companion's face. I knew it but had never really looked at her before. Her eyes were not quite black. The hair that escaped from underneath her hat was. A small scar ran along her cheekbone, toward the corner of one eye. She looked at me sporadically; the rest of the time, she stared out at the waves.

We dragged the life raft up onto the shore and started to walk. It felt uneasy to leave it there, bright orange against the desolate shore. An imprint of our brief presence. She walked with her face to the sky, to the summit of the mountain, and I kept my head down so as not to lose my footing on the uneven stones.

Though we were both practiced climbers, with no equipment the ascent was difficult and dangerous. After an hour we were halfway, and on a small shelf we stopped to catch our breath and look down. The water and shores were black, the ice white, the life raft garish orange. Distance turned it into an abstract painting. I could make out the boat but saw nobody on deck, and I wondered if they had retreated inside. I wondered if they had watched us leave.

She pulled her scarf from her mouth. "Can you feel it?" she asked. "It's almost like a sound."

I listened, and it crept upon me, a presence from somewhere above and behind us like a hum from the earth or the sky.

"They say there are places out here where the world is so sharp and thin it can be torn," she said, leaning toward me, quiet. The wind echoed her voice. Her eyes had turned black. "That there are other worlds beyond. It's easy to believe such things in such a place, don't you think?"

"That's what you think we're climbing toward?" I asked, and in reply received only an enigmatic smile.

At the end of our climb, we were both sweating and shivering, and I could taste something hot and sour in the air. My teeth and my heart ached. I saw my own longing reflected on her face, and the hum had risen to an electric swarm in my mind, silent and impossibly loud at the same time.

We followed a narrow path to the summit. A strangeness took hold of the landscape. My blood ran hot and then cold. A scouring wind tore down the passage, followed by gentle summer breezes, and even more disorienting were the sounds that assailed us—sighs and distant voices, mechanical screeching, the crackle of flame and the roar of a tide. I could no longer tell where we were. The world became abstract here, too, oddly smooth black rock like glass and patches of snow and a sky like gray water yawning above us. Alien constellations pinwheeled through it, bright and sharp.

I knew with sudden certainty that something had happened to this place to change it, and then I was certain of nothing, because we had reached the end of the path and before us stood the doorway.

It was even harder to see up close, but there was no mistaking what emerged from it. I heard the sea, not the iron mass we had spent the last month surrounded by, but the gentle breaking of surf against a shore. I could see nothing through it but had no doubt it was a doorway, a thin, sharp place, and the wind that flowed from it was not one I had ever felt before.

She took off her hat, and her hair blew loose. I did the same. We were no longer cold.

I reached for her hand, and we climbed up and through to the other side.

alien constellations pinwheeled
bright and sharp

Cloak of
Night

David Milley

Nights of new moon, when I was young, I left
my room to walk in dark. Taking the road
that led from town, I fled the light, went forth
blindly, bravely, until stars lit the path I strode.

The farther from people, the brighter the stars.
My eyes grew large; I saw fields grow bright.
Shadowless, I walked the shining road. No cars,
just galaxies of jewels set in the cloak of night.

Now the stars are almost gone. Those that remain
blink and sweep in lines across the lamplit sky.
The torches of our cities make all the heavens plain
and burn the firmament from light-blinded eyes.

But tonight, my life near done, I close my eyes and see
eight billion stars afire in the cloak of night around me.

Across the World

Eileen Lynch

The stars look different
where you are, looking
out at a corner of space
I can't see when I glance
up at the sky from my edge
of the Earth, but I sent you
a postcard, a photo taken
long ago, a rectangle
of dark sky by a camera too
old to have ever captured
burning bodies up above,
and on it I drew stars and
galaxies and constellations
that are all our own, so
when we look skyward
in unison to different palettes
of day and night and dusk
and dawn, at least we'll
always have one corner
of the sky that is wholly ours,
no matter where we are.

The State of Things Is This

Eileen Lynch

In the silence of the warmest of summer nights I can't help but feel a need to hold my breath, keep my lungs still beneath fingers splayed across tiny ribs, the slow ups and downs of life's constant flowing in my chest, through me, through us, a sacrilegious thing in air that seems not to move, as if the world in turn were holding its breath as well. If the world is still, then I will not be the one to disturb it, but then again, the Earth is spinning as we speak, continuing its lap around the sun and the stars—oh, the stars, as unmovable in the sky as they look, will shift like they're racing between the ends of the galaxy as the night wears on, and just down the road, a car makes the turn around the corner that will bring it home, and I'll take off running to meet it, just another part of a world in constant motion.

Late-Night Drives

Eileen Lynch

there are no streetlight sentinels
to watch over wanderers
on the roads that take us across
state lines, between shadows
shifting in the breeze, homes
and farms and trees swathed
in night's cloak, and in
the fields the fireflies
form galaxies of their own,
stars between stalks mirroring
the sky above.

the drive-through:
little more than counter
and kitchen in the oasis
of light across from dark
windows of a funeral home.
on this side of the street
we live life to the fullest,
all cold fingers
and sticky skin
and feeling warmth the day
soaked into the ground rising up
to meet us, even now, where we sit
on edges of car seats, doors open,
legs dangling over asphalt,
and there could be nothing more
to the world beyond this empty parking lot,
beyond the teenagers laughing
at the picnic table by the dumpster,
the hum of the cashier's radio.

we are our own little universe
of steel and leather and bodies and air
of you and me
(and ice cream)

driving home
we pull to the side of the road,
turn off headlights, and spare
a moment to count the fireflies
again, all the fleeting little
lights living fleeting little
lives compared to the stars
overhead, but they are all
beautiful in the vastness
of the dark, so let's stay a while
to watch and remember,
and hope for many more nights
like this one, in all the summers
yet to come.

all   the   fleeting   little   lights
living   fleeting   little   lives
compared to the stars overhead

Memory
> Sleep

Courtney Moody

It was the time when sky-parties
peak like whipped cream, when
stars are champagne droplets and
the moon laughs on her side and
cats roam through the house and,
if you have a gold net, you can
catch the Sandman in his prowl—

my mind drifted through a desert
of thoughts as a nomad in need of
a shower, picking up ten years of
atoms and molecules, and it stumbled
over dunes and sinkholes into you:

palm leaves in your hair like a crown,
eyelids hungover with dried chamomile.
You were a lighthouse growing from ash
before a triple chime announced your flame

because clocks run backward at 3 a.m.

This Sonnet's Label Was Peeled Off an 8-Track

Courtney Moody

Technology made fools to memory
as we clung to summer twenty-fourteen:

your eyes were tinted like cloud afternoons,
and I had sunrays braided in my hair.

You rewound my letters with a pencil
branded in toothmarks like a fossil.

Humidity mixed with playlists you sent;
all I could taste in the music was salt,

but a bottle of your soliloquies
helped masquerade dreams as reality.

We backdropped our lives with pins and photos
till paper edges blended with drywall.

We hoped that summer would rotate again
but I forgot—my Walkman died.

Days of 2019

Shira Haus

After Cavafy

He told me all his secrets next to the overgrown soccer field,
breath heavy with late summer and dollar-store wine.
He told me he was in love and didn't know what to do,
and I took another sip instead of answering,
let the alcohol sit on my tongue until the sting dissolved.

Lately, the ground had rolled uneasily under my feet
every time I took a step. I wanted to be ten years old
again, to roll down the hill and get grass stains
on my jeans. A sudden wind rustled the woods
behind us, the trees creaking like old bones.

I told him, eventually, that he should let it go,
and he gave a little laugh. He said I didn't
understand. My head was pillowed on his shoulder,
so I turned over and buried my face into the grass,
the moon's heavy eyes on the bareness of my neck.

I missed it all: the heady freedom of early summer,
the sand dunes, Lake Michigan shining like bright green
glass, fresh blackberry juice, the smell of crushed
dandelions. One by one, the days had slipped
like flickering minnows through my fingers.

Now, it was almost autumn, the air was showing signs
of the coming chill. I sat up, brushing off my shirt.
Some neighborhood kids were setting off firecrackers
in the street. They were shouting, their feet steady
and sure on the pavement. I could hear them laughing.

Late Nights at Susan's Roadhouse

Shira Haus

Bangor, Michigan

Midnight settles on the roadside diner,
sidewalk lit dimly by the blue neon sign.
Inside it would be quiet, save for the line cook,
who flirts with the waitress lighting a smoke.

The eggs are rubber, the coffee is tar,
but his jokes loosen the line of her mouth.
Querida, he says, *mi sueño, mi luz.*
She laughs, cigarette burning down to ash.

I am alone in my booth, arms sticking
to the red laminate, wondering when
I should interrupt to ask for the check.
A sweet strain of music from the kitchen

fades in. Jazz—Ella Fitzgerald, I think,
and I half-expect a rom-com moment,
the waitress and the line cook slow dancing,
their shoes squeaking on the grubby tile floor.

Across the room, another lone patron
flicks through his novel and frowns at the fly
buzzing over his head, not bothering
to swat it. He stretches out in his chair,

pulling at the collar of his flannel.
His wallet peeks from his jeans, stuffed with creased
photos of his family climbing the dunes.
We're in Michigan, so the wall's plastered

with sprawling maps, hand-drawn. Curlicue signs
proclaim our devotion to the lake, to
pure water that runs rusty in our pipes,
to South Haven seagulls and maple trees

tapped each spring for sap by men dressed in red
flannel. I sip my stale coffee, watching:
this state, its people, all surrounded by
our tiny oceans of fluorescent light.

surrounded by our tiny

oceans of fluorescent light

Time Capsule

Shira Haus

We are sitting on your father's porch and it is the middle
of the night and it is near the end of your life,
but neither of us knows that yet. Instead you
are trying your best to catch the fireflies that tease us
with their fleeting little lights, and I am watching you,
a study of sputtering porch light on dark hair.
Outside our fluorescent bubble, the driveway fades
into ink-black, and you squint, trying to see the end,
tossing one of the fireflies half-jokingly to see
if it will light up and pierce a hole in the darkness.

I Remember Us

Us

Jaime Dill

At fifteen, you don't know nothin'
Was the mantra of our elders
At thirty, I tend to agree
But one thing fifteen-year-old me knew
Was the sound of your car in the drive
The twisted wire coat hanger from my closet
Tying the muffler to the frame
Snarling with a death rattle
But somehow hanging on
I knew her quiet too
Five-speed engine clinking
In the August night
Parked on the gravel but
Listening to us meet
Our bodies on her faded red purple paint
As you point out the stars
And I believe every story you tell

I couldn't see that we were cliché
How we were a rendition of
All the young loves before us
I only saw how
You were everything I'd never known
And everything I wanted to learn

Est. 2005

Jaime Dill

We don't have that fancy sort
Of nostalgia, the kind where you
Vacation some place you honeymooned
Or buy new rings and repeat vows
We just drive to the gas station near
The state line, blasting country radio
And winning the lottery because
The little Mooresboro store
Still has the same ice cream
Vanilla, and cookie dough
Sometimes it's some unplanned errand
Puts us out on Andrew Mills Road
That old route that takes us between
Your mom's house and my folks
It's always near the bridge, the one
By the massive house no one
Lives in that used to make us see ghosts
There, I look at you or you at me
And we say over top of each other,
"My, it's been a long while since
We drove this way"
We arrive and we linger with
The gearshift in park, there
On the grassy spot you made bare
From years of parking beside dad's car
Instead of behind on the gravel
We stare out the windshield at the
Glowing windows of the home that
Made me, then made us
Talk about all the time
Since the Aprils of our youth
And laugh at jokes no one else
Could ever find funny

Kinetic Kindling

Jaime Dill

Campfire crackle ascending
Into obscure shifting shadow
The sky doesn't look the same
Freckled by embers, pin prick
Galaxies in flux before
Fizzling out into memory
Hypnotist crickets resurrect the dead
Evoking the spirit of every other neck
Craned back, wondering if
You can feel them
The way they feel you
Our DNA wafts up with the sparks
Coalesces in the firmament
To witness all we do
Without prejudice or partiality
Here in the stars, we are small
But hardly insignificant or few

Small World

Ben von Jagow

Weeknights that summer we piled into Riley's Sentra and drove, not to anywhere in particular though often enough we ended up at the quarry. Cole sometimes stole pot from his brother, and we'd smoke it there beneath the stars. No cars or city lights, just profiles bathed in moonlight. Someone, usually Riley or Hisko, would ask me to tell the BB story and I would.

More of an analogy than a story, it was our way to "conceptualize space," as Riley put it.

Shrink Earth down to the size of a BB, I'd start. Always wary of a group, it was easier for me to speak to the dark. *Pluto, the farthest planet in our solar system, would be the size of a red blood cell, a mile and a half away.* Pluto isn't a planet, Cole would say and someone would tell him to shut up.

So, Earth's the size of a BB. Our nearest star, Proxima Centauri, would be larger than an exercise ball, and more than 10,000 miles away.

Here's Earth. I'd lift a small BB-sized pebble even though it was too dark for anyone to see. *And our nearest star is in Australia.*

Often enough there was someone new and I'd pause to let their thoughts catch up. The boys had heard it all before and they knew the punches kept coming.

There are more than a hundred billion stars in the Milky Way galaxy.

Sometimes I'd have to cut to another analogy just to emphasize the sheer size of a billion.

Twelve days to count to one million.

Thirty-one years to count to one billion.

One hundred billion stars in the Milky Way. Of which we know one, orbited by nine planets. Eight, Cole would interject, and someone would tell him to shut up.

Hisko would play his part and talk about the moons, and people would listen because Hisko, indifferent to everything, was enthusiastic about the moons in our solar system. More than two hundred of them, he'd say. Then he'd go on about the atmosphere on Saturn's moon, Titan, and how scientists saw clouds and rivers and seas and so they assumed Titan had water but really it was methane, that clear liquid you find in those transparent dollar store lighters. Seas of methane.

And then Riley would cut in and say that the Milky Way was only one of more than one hundred billion other galaxies, and we'd sit in silence until Ghaddy would say what he always said.

Bullshit.

And if it was anyone other than Ghaddy we would've argued, but he was too stubborn and so we bit our lips and sulked in silence, unsure if we were upset because we forfeited the argument, or upset because our best friend's world was so small.

beneath the stars

no cars or city lights

Stars and Needles

Ben von Jagow

Out here, away from the glow of the city
stars like salt grains   lost in a black rug

the moon like a clipped nail
not a cloud in sight

side by side in the sand

sounds of the ocean, crashing waves
enough to drown shallow thoughts

I'm leaving tomorrow
the elephant hangs heavy
            like tar

you think we're alone? she asks

I almost look
what stops me is the philosophy in her voice
she isn't talking about beach dwellers

I follow the trail of the Milky Way
a method used by ancient hunters
one way to home
one way to oblivion

there are words we won't speak
questions we won't ask

no, I say
more to the stars than to her

Earth is spinning
night is a canvas

on cue, a brushstroke

make a wish, she says

I don't mention that they're not actually stars
just bits of debris burning up in the atmosphere
smaller than the sand grains on which we lie

better to let her believe
the universe is speaking

she grabs my hand
do you think one day we'll find something?
it's dark but I know where her eyes lie

I want to say it's too big
a trillion galaxies with a hundred billion stars
but words mean nothing

there's too much space to cover
like digging canyons with a needle

she senses the shift
my silence louder than the crashing waves

it takes a second for her to speak
her voice barely above a whisper

what if we're not the only ones searching?

like a needle to logic's balloon
the thought punctures

a satellite spans the sky, disappears
the sand beneath like a body cast

all that space to cover
          a daunting task, most definitely
but not insurmountable

and if one day, I decide to dig a canyon
with nothing more than the head of a needle
I might just rush to give her a call

because logic should tell me
when it comes to clearing space
that two heads
are certainly better than one.

Beach Night

Lotte van der Krol

The last night of the last summer we piled into a car and drove down to the beach, singing along to Springsteen songs, laughing at our knees pressed so close together in the backseat. The world was looming over us but tonight it was small enough to swallow. We rolled the windows down as we drove by the boardwalk carnival, the bright purple green blue lights pouring into our smiles, the blaring music and people's voices pouring into our veins. We sent our own voices and music back out in answer and laughed as the lights faded behind us, as we drove into the starry dark toward the dunes, as we drove away for one more night, away from tired eyes and heavy sighs, painful cupboard secrets and childhood drawings on the fridge, with memories and bottles and firewood rattling in the trunk. We sank our feet into the sand and built the fire up high so the night could never come close enough to strangle us. Arm in arm in arm in arm in arm we watched the distant carnival lights go out one by one till we were the only ones left in the dark, with the waves lapping and the stars shining and the fire burning and our hearts burning and we were alive and we were so free. We danced and sang and laughed and drank and forgot about who we had to be tomorrow, the packed cars and booked flights and inevitable goodbyes. The drinks and the fire burned in our veins and the endless stars burned in our smiles and the sand was soft beneath our bare feet and life was good and we would miss each other so, but not yet, not yet. The stars moved, our feet grew tired, the fire in our hearts died down. Too drunk and too happy to drive back home to our looming futures we made our beds in the sand beneath the fields of brilliant stars, talking for hours, our eyes never closing, already feeling homesick, already missing each other, even with our hands right there within reach. Already feeling time slipping through our fingers. Already struggling to stay. Desperate to stay. So we took pieces of our-selves and buried them in the sand, a lock of hair, a small dream, a shard of broken heart, tears never to be shed, a life never allowed to live, promising each other that even after the songs had finished, even after the sun had come up, even after we were long gone and had moved on to schools and jobs and a dream overseas and a fear come true and the same old same old, even after we barely remembered the drawings on the fridge and each others' names, we'd still be there. A part of us always beside the fire burning so high it reached the stars, beside the waves lapping endlessly at the shoreline, still singing and dancing and laughing and living and leaving and staying and and and

till one day the sea will wash it all away.

the   stars   shining
and   the   fire   burning
and our hearts burning
and   we   were   alive
and we were so free

Contributors

Jakky Bankong-Obi writes from Abuja, Nigeria. Jakky is co-editor at Ice Floe Press, and her work is forthcoming or published in *London Grip*, *The Kalahari Review*, *patchwork lit mag*, *Gutter Magazine*, *Hobart Pulp*, *Pidgeonholes*, *Memento: An Anthology of Contemporary Nigerian Poetry*, and elsewhere. Jakky enjoys long walks and yoga and dabbles in nature photography. Jakky is on Twitter at @jakkybeefive.

AJ Buckle is a poet and teacher living in and writing from his apartment in Ottawa, Canada. He holds an honors BA in literature and enjoys listening to records and tending to his houseplants when not having an existential crisis. His work has previously appeared in *The Broken City*, *Joypuke*, and *Capsule Stories Spring 2021 Edition*. You can read his dumb tweets at @buckle_aj or find him on Instagram at @ajbuckle1985.

Anna Caldwell is a speculative fiction writer based in East Anglia, United Kingdom. She holds a BA in English and creative writing from Coventry University and is working on her first novel.

Jaime Dill is an accomplished book coach, founder of Polish & Pitch editorial agency, and editor-in-chief of Cardigan Press who uses her precious downtime to pour her lesser-known self into free verse poetry. Jaime's writing reflects her professional interest in language while also ripping apart the rules to show the world the raw beauty of emotion and femininity. This is best seen in her debut *I Remember Us*, praised as "a time capsule of a relationship's most precious and sometimes painful moments." Learn more about Jaime and her various literary worlds at linktr.ee/jaime_dill.

Victoria Schofield Dobbs is an MFA candidate at the University of North Carolina Wilmington and the Young Voices Editor for *Chautauqua.*

Sarah Ernestine was raised in the southern United States but currently lives in London, where she is studying to get her MA in publishing. She loves finding the juncture of art and literature, writing mostly poetry and creative nonfiction. Her writing has previously been featured in *Inverted Syntax* and *Better than Starbucks.*

Shira Haus is a student at Allegheny College studying English, Spanish, and political science. Her work has been published in *The Albion Review, Snapdragon Journal,* and *Oakland Arts Review.* In her free time, she likes to read, cook, and knit while daydreaming about herding sheep in the mountains. You can find her on Instagram at @goldenapplepoems.

Aral L. is a nineteen-year-old nonbinary latinx poet living in Canada. They are currently a student and have dreamed of being a writer since they were young. They have released a chapbook titled *17.*

Stella Lei (she/her) is a teen writer whose work is published or forthcoming in *Gone Lawn, Milk Candy Review, FEED,* and elsewhere. She is an editor in chief for *The Augment Review,* and she tweets at @stellalei04.

Joyce Liu is a teenage poet from Ottawa, Canada. When she's not writing, she can be found taking long walks in the woods and watching Formula 1 races. More of her work can be found in released and upcoming issues of *perhappened*, *FEED*, and *Burning Jade Literary and Arts Magazine*.

Eileen Lynch is a writer, yarn hoarder, and the author of a handful of short stories in various zines and anthologies. If you're interested in seeing where her writing ends up next, you can find her online at @eileenpdf on Twitter.

Isabella J Mansfield writes about anxiety, grief, body image, intimacy, and the human condition. Mansfield has performed at The Oberon Theatre (Cambridge, Massachusetts), Nambucca (London, UK), and at various readings and open mics across the US. Her poems have been featured by *The Wild Word*, *Sad Girl Review*, *Liminality*, *Capsule Stories*, and *East Jasmine Review*, as well as in publications by Augie's Bookshelf and Rebel Mountain Press. In 2017, she was a Brittany Noakes Award semifinalist. She won the 2018 Mark Ritzenhein New Author Award. Finishing Line Press published her Pushcart Prize-nominated chapbook, *The Hollows of Bone*, in 2019. She lives in Howell, Michigan, with her family.

Natalie Marino is a poet, physician, and mother. Her work appears in *Barren Magazine*, *Capsule Stories*, *Dust Poetry Magazine*, *Literary Mama*, *MORIA*, *Re-Side*, and elsewhere. She also reads poetry submissions for *Bracken Magazine*. She lives in Thousand Oaks, California, with her husband and two daughters.

Matthew Miller teaches social studies, swings tennis rackets, and writes poetry—all hoping to create home. He and his wife live beside a dilapidated orchard in Indiana, where he tries to shape dead trees into playhouses for his four boys. His poetry has been featured in *River Mouth Review, Club Plum*, and *Ekstasis Magazine*. Find him online at mattleemiller.wixsite.com/poetry.

David Milley (he/him) has written and published verse since the 1970s, while working at a career as a technical writer and web applications developer. His work has appeared in *Painted Bride Quarterly, Christopher Street*, and *Bay Windows*. Retired now, David lives in southern New Jersey with his husband of four decades, Warren Davy, who's made his living as a farmer, woodcutter, nurseryman, beekeeper, and cook. These days, Warren tends his garden and keeps honeybees, while David walks and writes.

Thomas J. Misuraca studied writing, publishing, and literature at Emerson College in Boston before moving to Los Angeles. Over ninety-five of his short stories and two novels have been published. Most recently, his story "Giving Up the Ghosts" was published in *Constellations* and nominated for a Pushcart Prize. He is also a multi-award-winning playwright with over 135 short plays and eleven full-lengths produced globally. His musical *Geeks!* was produced off Broadway in May 2019.

Courtney Moody is an honor medallion graduate of the University of Central Florida with a BA in creative writing. In 2018, she was awarded the Promising Scholar Award by UCF's English Department. Her poetry can be found or is forthcoming in the YellowJacket Press anthology *Chasing Light, The Cypress Dome*, and *Bridge*. Her prose can be found online in *Bridge Eight*.

Pamela Nocerino's life is full of creative play. She writes, acts, teaches, and once helped build a giant troll in the Rocky Mountains. Armed with a BA in theater arts and an MA in communication, Pamela enjoyed a brief career on stage in Denver until she needed health insurance. Then she taught in public schools for over twenty years and raised two sons. One of her new short plays will be staged at The Grand Theatre in 2021, and another was performed online with Denver's Theater 29. Her poems were selected recently for *Plum Tree Tavern* and Splintered Disordered Press, and her ghostwriting income is a lifeline in these need-so-much-chocolate times.

Vic Nogay is a proud Ohioan writing to explore her traumas and misremembrances. Her work appears or is forthcoming in *Lost Balloon, Emerge Literary Journal, perhappened, Little Engines, Ellipsis Zine*, and others. She tweets at @vicnogay. Read more at linktr.ee/vicnogay.

Emily L. Pate is a writer, avid traveler, and collector/oversharer of bizarre facts. Born and raised in California, she holds an MFA in creative writing from the University of British Columbia. Her poetry and travel writing have appeared in *The Rising Phoenix Review, Funicular Magazine*, and *Willawaw Journal*, among others. She can be found at emilylpate.com.

Mallory Pearson is an artist and writer living in Queens, New York. She writes about themes of folklore, femininity, and loss, and how these elements interact with the Southern United States.

Emily Polson holds a BFA in creative writing from Belhaven University and has been published in *Catfish Creek*, *FEED*, *433 Magazine*, and *The Brogue*. Originally from Central Iowa, she now lives in Brooklyn and works in book publishing. You can follow her on Twitter at @emilycpolson.

Ismim Putera is a poet and writer from Sarawak, Malaysia. His works have appeared in *Ghostheart Literary Journal*, *Ayaskala*, *Prismatica Magazine*, *Orris Root Science and Art Literary Magazine*, *Eksentrika*, and elsewhere.

Diana Raab, PhD, is an award-winning memoirist, poet, blogger, speaker, and author of ten books and over 1,000 articles and poems. She's also editor of two anthologies, *Writers on the Edge: 22 Writers Speak about Addiction and Dependency* and *Writers and Their Notebooks*. Raab's two memoirs are *Regina's Closet: Finding My Grandmother's Secret Journal* and *Healing with Words: A Writer's Cancer Journey*. She blogs for *Psychology Today*, *Thrive Global*, *Sixty and Me*, and *Wisdom Daily* and is a frequent guest blogger for other sites. Her two latest books are *Writing for Bliss: A Seven-Step Plan for Telling Your Story* and *Transforming Your Life* and *Writing for Bliss: A Companion Journal*. Visit dianaraab.com.

Jessica Rapisarda earned her MFA from Hollins University. Her poetry, essays, and literary reviews have been published in *jubilat*, *The Potomac Review*, *Grace and Gravity*, *The Establishment*, *Huff Post*, and more. She teaches writing at Northern Virginia Community College, where she is on the editorial board of *The Northern Virginia Review*.

Alice Rogers is a Welsh writer recently graduated with an MSc in creative writing from The University of Edinburgh. They specialize in American historical fiction with LGBT+ themes.

Holly Ruskin (she/her) has been a writer all her life but started exploring the poetic form after the birth of her daughter in 2019. She graduated with a BA in English literature and film and went on to complete an MA in film, specializing in feminism and the representation of women. As a lecturer and freelance writer, she has edited screenplays and written short stories and academic essays. But it is writing poems about motherhood that has brought her the most creative joy. She cofounded *blood moon poetry*, an inclusive and welcoming place for female poets to submit their work for publication. A selection of her work is published in an anthology of stories about postnatal depression titled *Not the Only One*, and her poems have been published in various zines, anthologies, and journals. She also writes for *Harness Magazine* and is a *Motherscope* contributor. Holly lives in Bristol, United Kingdom. She can be found on Instagram at @mother.in.motion.

Rebecca Ruvinsky is a student, poet, and emerging writer in Orlando, Florida. She has kept a streak of writing a poem every day since 2016, with work published or forthcoming in *Wizards in Space*, *Sylvia Magazine*, *Underland Arcana*, *Funicular Magazine*, *From the Farther Trees*, *dreams walking*, *Floresta Magazine*, and others. She loves baking cookies, watching rocket launches, and listening to music too loud. She can be found at @writeruvinsky.

Sher Ting has lived in Singapore for most of her life before moving to Australia for medical school. She has work published or forthcoming in anthologies, including *Byline Legacies* and *Pages Penned in Pandemic*, and literary magazines, including *Eunoia Review, opia, Overheard,* and *Interstellar Literary Review.* She is currently an editor of *The Aurora Journal* and a poetry reader for *Farside Review.* She tweets at @sherttt and writes at downintheholocene.wordpress.com.

Taylor Wyna Stewart is a writer from Birmingham, Alabama, whose work has been featured in *Cypress Press, Aura Literary Arts Review,* and *Reckon Women.* Taylor serves as the founder and editor in chief of *Camellias,* a Southern regional magazine dedicated to the modern Southern woman. Say "hi" on Twitter and Instagram at @TayyWyna.

Lotte van der Krol's favorite color is the green-blue of the sky on a clear day about an hour after the sun has set. Her short fiction has appeared in *Popshot Quarterly* and *The Cabinet of Heed,* and you can find more of her stories on lottevanderkrol.wordpress.com. She's also way too much on Twitter at @lottevdkrol.

Kristin Van Tassel teaches writing and American literature at Bethany College in Lindsborg, Kansas. She writes essays and poetry about place, teaching, motherhood, and travel. Her work has appeared in literary, academic, and travel publications, including *The Chronicle of Higher Education, World Hum, ISLE, The Journal of Ecocriticism, Los Angeles Review of Books, Wraparound South, Temenos, Burningword Literary Journal,* and *About Place.*

Ben von Jagow is a writer and poet from Ottawa who lives in Cape Town, South Africa. His work has been featured in literary journals such as *Amsterdam Quarterly*, *Marathon Literary Review*, *The Stockholm Review of Literature*, *Newfoundland Quarterly*, and *Literary Review of Canada*, among others. For more of Ben's work, visit benvj.com.

Madison Zehmer is a poet and wannabe historian from North Carolina with published and forthcoming work in *Déraciné Magazine*, *Drunk Monkeys*, *Gone Lawn*, *LandLocked Magazine*, and elsewhere. She is editor in chief of *Mineral Lit Mag* and a reader for *Lily Poetry Review*. Her first chapbook, *Unhaunting*, will be released by Kelsay Books in 2021.

Editorial Staff

Natasha Lioe, Founder and Publisher

Natasha Lioe graduated with a BA in narrative studies from University of Southern California. She's always had an affinity for words and stories and emotions. Her work has appeared in *Adsum Literary Magazine*, and she won the Edward B. Moses Creative Writing Competition in 2016. Her greatest strength is finding and focusing the pathos in an otherwise cold world, and she hopes to help humans tell their unique, compelling stories.

Carolina VonKampen, Publisher and Editor in Chief

Carolina VonKampen graduated with a BA in English and history from Concordia University, Nebraska and completed the University of Chicago's editing certificate program. She is available for hire as a freelance copyeditor and book designer. For more information on her freelance work, visit carolina vonkampen.com. Her writing has appeared in *So to Speak*'s blog, *FIVE:2:ONE*'s #thesideshow, *Moonchild Magazine*, and *Déraciné Magazine*. Her short story "Logan Paul Is Dead" was nominated by *Dream Pop Journal* for the 2018 Best of the Net. She tweets about editing at @carolinamarie_v and talks about books she's reading on Instagram at @carolinamariereads.

April Bayer, Reader

April Bayer is an MA student in English literature at the University of South Dakota. She graduated with high distinction from Concordia University, Nebraska in 2019 with a BA in English and theology and a BS Ed in educational studies. When she isn't busy teaching her students about literature and composition, she enjoys writing poetry, playing with cats, and researching the works of Willa Cather. Her work has previously appeared in *Potpourri* and *Capsule Stories Isolation Edition*. April joined *Capsule Stories* as a reader in November 2020.

Stephanie Coley, Reader

Stephanie Coley is a country girl from Gering, Nebraska. She graduated in 2016 from Concordia University, Nebraska with a BA in English and a minor in art. She has been a journalism teacher, janitor, data technician, and more. Stephanie is a published poet, appearing in the National Creativity Series of 2009 and *Mango* Issue 3, Respeto, in 2017. She is also a winner of the 2020 Historic Posters Reimagined Project, which can be found at the Nebraska History Museum in Lincoln, Nebraska. Stephanie currently works as the program manager at the West Nebraska Arts Center in Scottsbluff, Nebraska. Stephanie joined *Capsule Stories* as a reader in January 2021.

Rhea Dhanbhoora, Reader

Rhea Dhanbhoora worked for close to a decade as an editor and writer before quitting her job and moving to New York to get her master's degree and finally writing the stories everyone told her no one would ever read. Her work has appeared or is forthcoming in publications such as *Sparkle & Blink*, *Awakened Voices*, *Five on the Fifth*, *Capsule Stories Autumn 2020 Edition*, *Fly on the Wall Press*, *HerStry*, *Artsy*, *Broccoli Mag*, and *JMWW*. Her work has been nominated for a Pushcart Prize and Best American Essays. She is currently on the board of directors for the literary organization Quiet Lightning and editor of RealBrownTalk. Rhea joined *Capsule Stories* as a reader in January 2021. She's working on several projects, including a linked story collection about women based in the underrepresented Parsi Zoroastrian diaspora. You can read her work online at rheadhanbhoora.com.

Hannah Fortna, Reader

Hannah Fortna graduated in 2016 from Concordia University, Nebraska, combining her passion for the written word and her affinity for art making with a degree in English and a minor in photography. After a three-year career as a freelance copyeditor, she heard traveling calling her name and now works seasonal jobs in places connected to America's national parks. When she's not selling souvenirs to tourists in gift shops, she enjoys hiking, photographing natural spaces, and writing about the flora and fauna she saw while on the trail. She reads anything from poetry to middle-grade novels, but the nature-inspired creative nonfiction section is her haunt in any bookstore. Her poetry has previously appeared in *Moonchild Magazine* and *Capsule Stories Spring 2019 Edition*. Hannah joined *Capsule Stories* as a reader in November 2020.

Kendra Nuttall, Reader

Kendra Nuttall is a copywriter by day and poet by night. She has a BA in English with an emphasis in creative writing from Utah Valley University. Her work has previously appeared in *Spectrum*, *Capsule Stories*, *Chiron Review*, and *What Rough Beast*, as well as various other journals and anthologies. She is the author of the poetry collection *A Statistical Study of Randomness* (Finishing Line Press, 2021). Kendra lives in Utah with her husband and poodle. When she's not writing, you can find her hiking, watching reality TV, or attempting to pet every animal she sees. You can find out more about her work at kendranuttall.com. Kendra joined *Capsule Stories* as a reader in January 2021.

Rachel Skelton, Reader

Rachel Skelton graduated from William Woods University with a BA in English, a concentration in writing, and a secondary major in business administration, a concentration in management. She has interned for Dzanc Books and now works as a freelance fiction editor specializing in speculative fiction. You can find more information about her work at theeditingskeleton.com. She occasionally tweets about editing at @EditingSkeleton and talks about books she's reading at @TheReadingSkeleton on Instagram. When she's not doing anything reading-related, she's hanging out with her cats, collecting houseplants, and attempting to learn how to crochet. Rachel joined *Capsule Stories* as a reader in January 2021.

Deanne Sleet, Reader

Deanne Sleet is a graduate of Saint Louis University with a BA in English, a concentration in creative writing, and minors in African American studies and women's and gender studies. She has interned for *River Styx* and Midwest Artist Project Services, where she gained experience with grant writing, editing, and writing copy. She is currently the leasing and marketing manager at City Lofts on Laclede and holds the secretary position for SLU's Black Alumni Association. She writes short fiction and poetry, and a novel is in the making. In her spare time, she hangs out with her cat and roller-skates. Deanne joined *Capsule Stories* as a reader in February 2021.

Claire Taylor, Reader

Claire Taylor is a writer in Baltimore, Maryland, where she lives with her husband, son, and a bossy old cat. Her writing has appeared in a variety of publications and has received nominations for the Pushcart Prize and Best American Short

Stories. Claire's first publication at age ten in *Highlights Magazine* was a poem about what it might feel like to be a leaf. Nowadays, her work focuses largely on themes of motherhood and mental illness. In addition to writing for adults, Claire is the creator of Little Thoughts, a monthly newsletter of stories and poetry for children, and she has written several picture books that are searching for publishing homes. A selection of Claire's work is available online at clairemtaylor.com. Claire joined *Capsule Stories* as a reader in March 2021.

Submission
Guidelines

Capsule Stories **is a print literary magazine** published once every season. Our first issue was published on March 1, 2019, and we accept submissions year-round.

Become published in a literary magazine run by like-minded people. We have a penchant for pretty words, an affinity to the melancholy, and an undeniably time-ful aura. We believe that stories exist in a specific moment, and that that moment is what makes those stories unique.

What we're really looking for are stories that can touch the heart. Stories that come from the heart. Stories about love, identity, the self, the world, the human condition. Stories that show what living in this world as the human you are is like.

We accept short stories, poems, and remarkably written essays. For short stories and essays, we're interested in pieces under 3000 words. You may include up to five poems in a single poetry submission, and please send only one story or essay at a time. Please send previously unpublished work only, and only submit to one category at a time. Simultaneous submissions are okay, but please let us know if your submission is accepted elsewhere. Please include a brief third-person bio with your submission, and attach your submission in a Word document (no PDFs, please!).

Find our full submission guidelines and current theme descriptions at capsulestories.com/submissions. You can email your submission to us at submissions@capsulestories.com.

Connect with us!
capsulestories.com
@CapsuleStories on Twitter and Facebook
@CapsuleStoriesMag on Instagram